# I'm Reading About

# NEW MEXICO

## Land of Enchantment!

GALLOPADE

by Carole Marsh

Printed and Manufactured in Peachtree City, GA., USA
www.gallopade.com

Book design: John Hanson

Editorial manager: Janice Baker

New Mexico is a great state.

It is one of a kind.

What makes New Mexico special?

Let's read about it

and see!

# NATIVE AMERICANS

Who lived in New Mexico first?

Native Americans did!

They moved around to find food.
They hunted for animals to eat.
They fished in New Mexico's rivers.
They gathered fruits and seeds and nuts.

Some of the first explorers came to New Mexico in 1540.
They came from the country of Spain.

Francisco de Coronado was their leader.
He and his men were looking for cities of gold!

# SETTLEMENT

A man named Juan de Oñate traveled north from Mexico in 1598. He started the first settlement in New Mexico. He named it San Juan de los Caballeros. That name means "Saint John of the Knights."

Juan de Oñate came to New Mexico with 500 settlers.

# San Juan de los Caballeros

# STATEHOOD

New Mexico was the 47th state
to join the United States of America!

Isn't it great,
to be a state!
I bet New Mexico
could hardly wait!

New Mexico became a state in 1912.

New Mexico
The 47th State
Here we are!

# FLAG

I am the state flag.
I was adopted in 1925.

What colors am I?
Yellow and red.

Look at me.
What else do you see?

I fly high over the state of New Mexico!

# CAPITAL

Say hello to Santa Fe,
the capital city of New Mexico!

There is an important building in Santa Fe.
It is the State Capitol.
New Mexico's laws are made there!

# Capitol

# SEAL

I am a seal,
but I am not the State Seal.
If I were, I would be very important.
I would be stamped on many official papers.
*(Ouch, that might hurt!)*

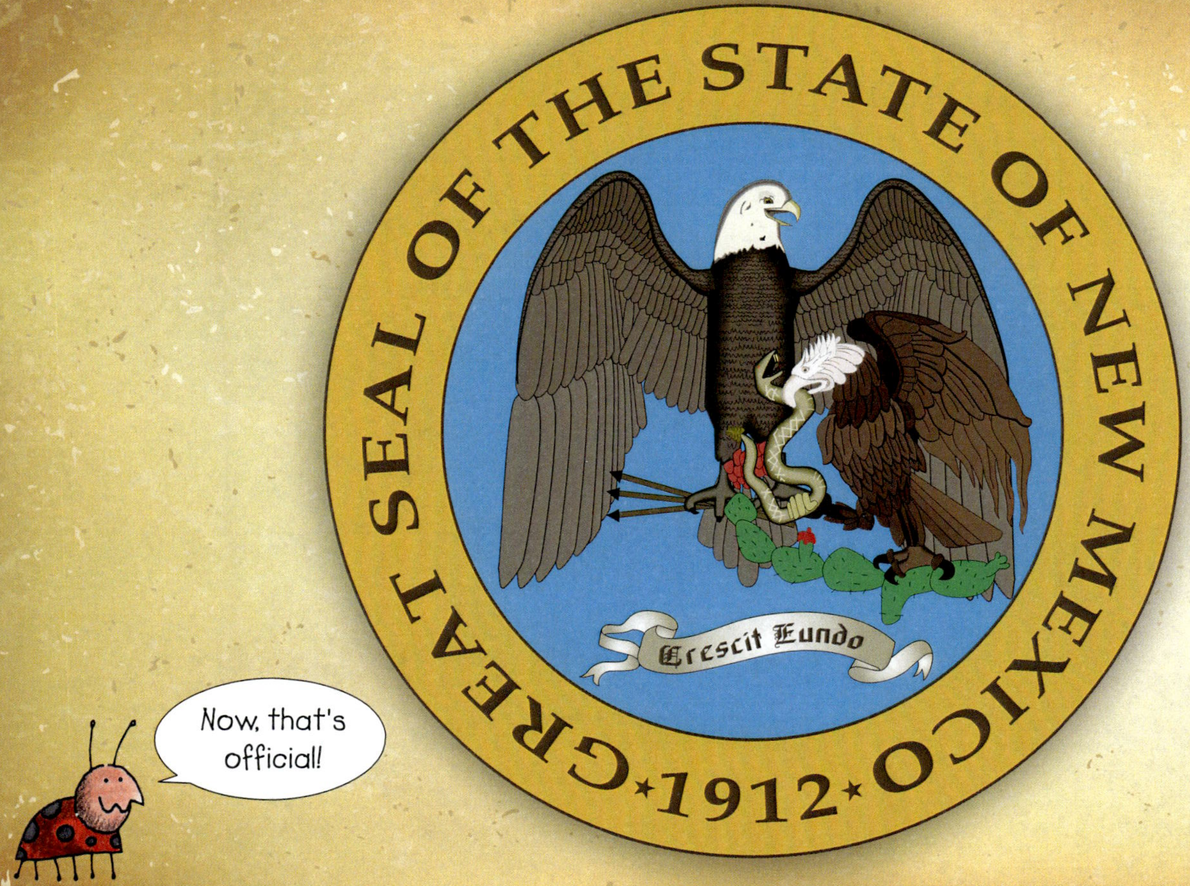
GREAT SEAL OF THE STATE OF NEW MEXICO ★ 1912 ★
Crescit Eundo
Now, that's official!

# NICKNAME

State nicknames are fun!
State nicknames are great!
They share fun facts
about each state!

New Mexico's nickname is "Land of Enchantment."

New Mexico is known for its beautiful land and interesting history!

# Land of Enchantment

# BORDERS

Look at New Mexico.
New Mexico is in a region called "the Southwest."

New Mexico borders four other states.
It also borders the country of Mexico.
Find New Mexico and its neighbors on the map!

# Borders

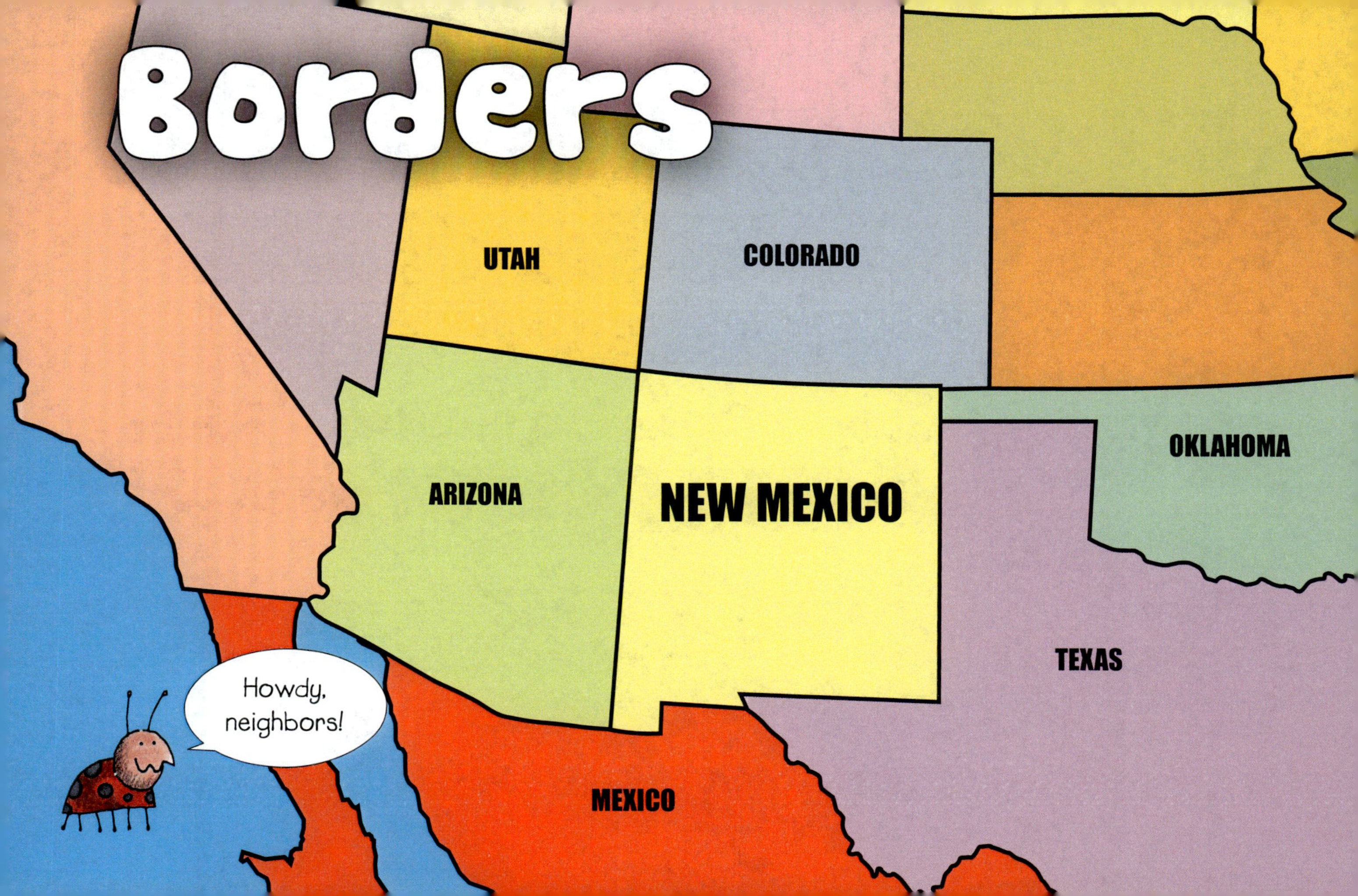
UTAH
COLORADO
OKLAHOMA
ARIZONA
NEW MEXICO
TEXAS
Howdy, neighbors!
MEXICO

# COUNTIES

New Mexico is divided into 33 counties.
Counties are a form of local government.
Counties provide services that people need!
Those services include:

**Schools** **Parks** **Libraries** **Police**
**Firefighters** **and More!**

# Counties

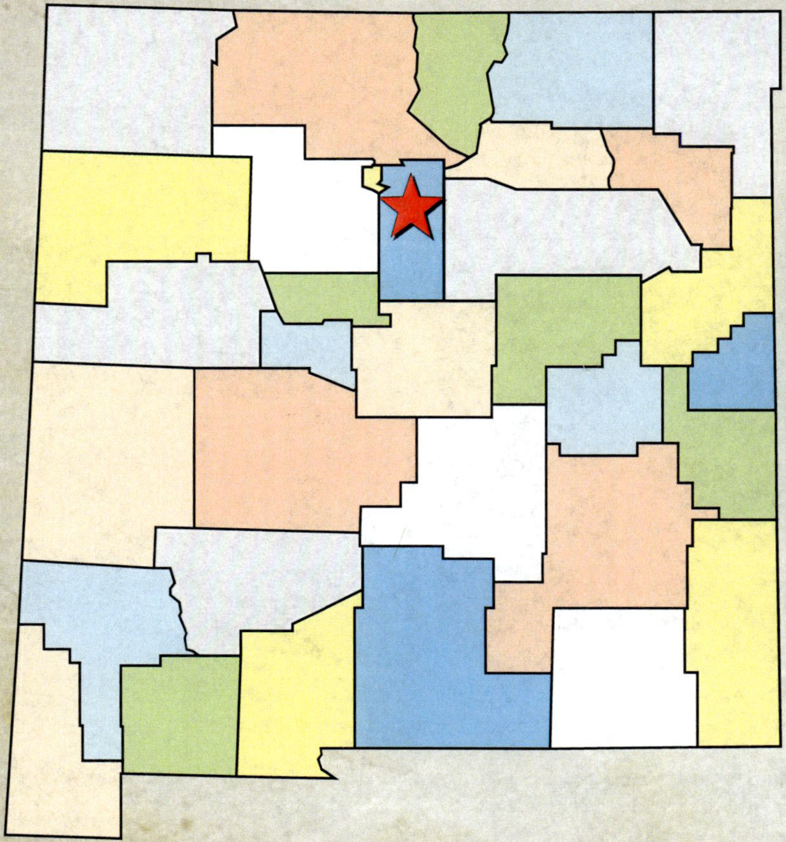

NEW MEXICO'S CAPITAL, SANTA FE, IS IN SANTA FE COUNTY.

PEOPLE

# Many famous people

**Conrad Hilton**
Founded Hilton Hotels

**William Hanna**
Animator who created *Yogi Bear* and *The Flintstones* cartoons

**Dolores Huerta**
Activist for the rights of farm workers and women

# PEOPLE

## Call our state home!

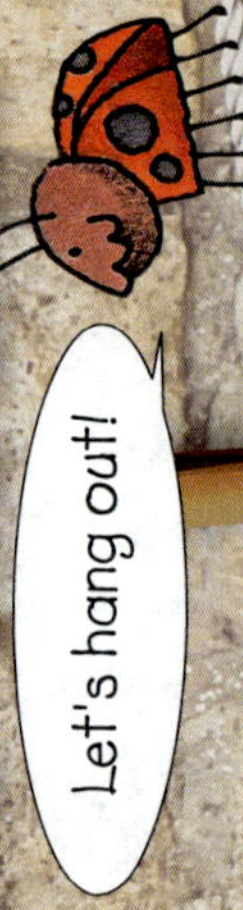

**Jeff Bezos**
Founder of Amazon.com

**Janet Napolitano**
First female U.S. Secretary of Homeland Security

**John Denver**
Singer and songwriter

# Greater Roadrunner

# BIRD

I am the state bird, and I fly
over New Mexico, proud and high.

As I fly, up in the sky,
I flap my wings to tell you "Hi!"

The New Mexico state bird is the Greater Roadrunner.

# Yucca

# FLOWER

I am the Yucca.
I am the state flower.

I grow where it's warm and sunny.
I bloom in summer and fall.
I help make New Mexico beautiful!

Look at me! Smell me!
My flowers grow on a long stalk!

# Piñon Pine

# TREE

I am a Piñon Pine—I'm the state tree.
All over New Mexico is where to find me.

My roots run deep, they keep me strong.
My leaves stay green, all year long.

I stand up straight, big and tall.
Don't climb too high—it would hurt to fall!

Tarantula Hawk Wasp

# INSECT

I am the Tarantula Hawk Wasp.
I am the state insect.

I am one of the biggest wasps.
My sting can really hurt!

I fly from flower to flower.
I am looking for nectar to drink.

BZZZZZZZZZZ!

# Deserts

# DESERTS

Let's go to the desert!

The desert is dry.
It hardly ever rains.

Temperatures are hot during the day
but cool off at night!

New Mexico's deserts are home to many animals:

**Scorpions** **Coyotes** **Snakes** **Tarantulas** **Hawks** **and More!**

Rocky Mountains

# MOUNTAINS

New Mexico's Rocky Mountains are the place to be.
Hiking, fishing, camping—
—fun for you and me.

If you were to climb
to the top of a tree,
you'd have a very nice view to see!

# Rio Grande

# RIVER

The Rio Grande is one of the longest rivers
in North America!
It flows through New Mexico.

This river habitat is home to many animals:

**Birds Deer Snakes Frogs Bats and More!**

The Rio Grande flows through
the city of Albuquerque.

# White Sands National Monument

# LANDMARK

Imagine a beach with no ocean.
That is what the White Sands National Monument looks like!

The White Sands have hills called sand dunes.
The sand is unique because it is made of gypsum.
Gypsum is a type of mineral.

The White Sands dunes move!
The sand is blown around by the wind.

# New Mexico Crops

# AGRICULTURE

New Mexico has many farms.
Why?
Because New Mexico has good soil and a warm climate!

Some of the top crops grown in New Mexico are:

**Pecans** **Hay** **Onions** **Chili Peppers**

Hey!
Don't forget about me!
I am a New Mexico cow.
I produce lots of milk to make dairy products!

# Sports in New Mexico

# SPORTS

Baseball! Basketball! Football!
New Mexico has it all.

Whether you like to watch or play,
You are sure to have a ball!

**Lobos** **Aggies** **Mustangs**

**Greyhounds**

**Cowboys**

**& More!**

# New Mexico: Home of Carlsbad Caverns

# CLAIM TO FAME

The Carlsbad Caverns are caves in the desert! The caverns are made up of underground rooms. The rooms are filled with stalactites, stalagmites, and even an underground lake!

All of the caverns have a name. Some names include the Balloon Ballroom, the King's Palace, and the Lake of the Clouds!

# GLOSSARY

**activist:** a person who takes action to promote some type of change

**climate:** weather conditions in an area over a long period of time

**habitat:** a place where plants or animals naturally live

**laws:** rules made by the government

**region:** an area that has similar characteristics

**settlement:** the first community in an area

**spelunking:** exploring caves

**stalactite:** a structure that hangs like an icicle from the roof of a cave

**stalagmite:** a column rising from the floor of a cave

**stalk:** the main stem of a plant